SURVIVING THE LOSS

OF A

LOVED ONE

Surviving the Loss of a Loved One

Surviving the Loss of a Loved One

ISBN: 9780967931227

Dedication

This book is dedicated to the memory of my husband and best friend Roosevelt "Ted" Harris and to all who have experienced and those yet to experience the loss of a loved one.

Also dedicated to my former pastors Melvin & April Jackson, Henry & Alicia Pigee', my children Denzil, Chisa, Damien & Ashley, family and friends that stood by and supported me during one of the most difficult times of my life and to my current pastors Sheridan E. & First Lady LarLeslie McDaniel.

Your continued prayers, patience and support will always be appreciated and never forgotten.

Introduction

No healthy, emotionally stable person enjoys thinking about death. Though inevitable it is an uncomfortable subject, one we would rather not discuss or experience. But as a part of life and (unless we live till the Rapture) we are sure to die and so it is with those we love.

Grief is a natural reaction to any important loss. It is a healthy, human response to situations such as: the death of a loved one, separation or divorce, miscarriage, injury or disability, the loss of a job, property or pet and children leaving home. Often the greatest loss we experience is the loss of a loved one. Loss through death is a painful experience but the pain does subside as you will discover through reading this book.

Everyone experiences loss or change at some time in life. Grieving is important because it is a part of the healing process. We cannot make an appointment or make a deal with death even though we each have an appointed time to die. More importantly for the Believer, is our Salvation which we receive without fee but simply through our belief and acceptance of Jesus Christ as our Savior as we find in Romans 10:9, *"That if thou shalt confess with thy mouth the Lord Jesus, and shalt believe in thine heart that God hath raised him from the dead, thou shalt be saved."*

This book is not for theological debates but moreover to help Christians go through and survive the grieving process. Its purpose is to help you face the loss, grieve the loss in a healthy manner and survive rising healed and victorious. It helps to have some Word deposited in you so you can make withdrawals during times of bereavement. As stated by the writer to the Hebrews, the truth that **it is appointed for men to die once, but after this the judgment** is an indisputable principle. (David Guzik Commentary)

Though it was not really the point of the writer to the Hebrews to discuss reincarnation, he certainly and completely *denies* it here.

We do not die and live and die and live, and some numbers of lives down the road face an eternal reckoning. This life is it, and then we face judgment. This means that *there are no second chances beyond the grave. Now* is the time to choose for Jesus Christ, because when we **die**, it is simply **after this the judgment**. "And as it is appointed unto men once to die, but after this the judgment:" Hebrews. 9:27, (David Guzik Commentary)

It is impressionable to see the 21ˢᵗ Century church striving to meet the "whole" need of its people. We do not always have the resources to minister to all the problems parishioners may encounter but we have the intellect to find an acceptable source that does. We serve a God who all knows, all powerful and everywhere at the same time and He supplies all our need even through counseling. We are employing those who have educationally mastered in areas of counseling so parishioners can be counseled from a practical, professional and Christian perspective.

This book is simply my experience with the death of my husband. It is a collection of notes made of my true emotions and survival techniques that made the difference between sanity and insanity.

God is so awesome. Writing this book allowed me to leap into the very depth and core of my own grief. I first recognized my own struggles and then was encouraged to face the various emotions manifested during this time.

There are unexpected responses you may get from friends and "family," that will knock your socks off if you are not rooted and grounded in the Word. It is said people are the biggest fools during weddings and funerals and I concur.

Under whatever circumstance you may be facing with someone's demise, I pray you can yet see God's hand on your life. You can yet feel him consoling, feel him carrying and nurturing you through this experience.

I realized some time ago that most of our uncomfortable, embarrassing and painful experiences are not just for us but to be used to positively minister to others. If we can pass through the grieving process in a healthy manner we can heal and effectively minister to others. Enjoy and be encouraged.

Table of Contents

Chapter 1
THE BEGINNING OF THE END

Eleven years seems brief when compared to the nineteen years of my previous marriage, especially since the eleven years were the best of my life. Recalling the wedding as though it were yesterday we married within six-weeks of our engagement. It finally happened after two failed marriages I had met the man of my dreams. God had finally hooked me up with my Boaz. The relationship was so superbly wonderful it alarmed me at times. My negative experiences from previous relationships had me waiting for the ball to drop. I was wounded in a prior marriage and did not heal properly. Consequently I was trying to get as much happiness I could from this marriage before it failed, before he did something stupid to ruin it all…like times before.

Ted proved to be different, he lined up with the Word; *Prov. 18:22 he who find a wife findeth a good thing and obtaineth favor of the Lord.* His characteristics were that of a prince in a fairy tale. A godsend, loving, polite, respectful, intelligent, resourceful, compatible mate and I could go on endlessly. Our interests were phenomenal we took pleasure in like things. Everyday felt as though we were on our honeymoon. We were so alike we would speak what the other was thinking at the same time. We were good together like peaches and cream.

His passing was though the world had stopped spinning on its axis or me trying to awake from a tumultuous dream. What? How? Why? All was running through my mind at the same time, thoughts of confusion and wonderment bouncing off one another. "Nah girl, wake up! God brought you through this before…he will do it again! Dead! Ted dead! Nope, not having it! Wake up now this is not funny, it is actually very troubling." But I was awake and I did receive the call from his nurse.

Most of the workers in the skilled nursing facility were Filipino with broken English but they were nice. The phone rang as I was dressing to make my daily visit on a Saturday morning. I answered and the caller said, "Mrs. Shiela Harris?" (Chila Haredis) is how it sounded. I replied, "Yes, this is she." "This is Yvonne from Country Villa and I am calling to tell you your husband passed away at 7:05 this morning." I said nothing. I was trying to process the statement hoping I misunderstood somehow. She repeated it. I replied, "OK…thank you." She asked who was to pick him up and I said I would call the mortuary.

From that moment I began to function on auto pilot, unable to cry and could barely think of what to do next. As I made calls, family and friends rushed to be by my side. My Pastors drove 70 miles one way to see about me and made the arrangements for the use of a larger church for the services and on behalf of the church also made a large donation towards the burial need. Friends and family came from everywhere bringing donations, food, words of comfort. God knew I needed it.

About three years into our marriage I became ill and took early retirement from my job of 30 years. The needed years of service were covered but not the age so I worked until age 50 actually retiring on my 50th birthday. With me retired and he disabled our income suffered severely. We had to change our lifestyle to the point of filing bankruptcy to get out from under the weight of our debt. In doing this, we let life insurances lapse and payments on burial plans ceased.

Shortly after this time Ted received a nice sum of money from a settlement. One of the things he did was purchased tandem burial property including fees for opening and closing and name plates. What lacked was money for the mortuary services and casket. Praise God I was referred to a young bass player who crossed our paths in church who also worked in a mortuary as a mortician. He picked up the body and I had no money to give him. Climbing down out of the denial tree I called him one week before Ted passed away and my eldest son and I met with him to talk about the cost. Their prices were phenomenally reasonable. When I called him he told me, "Don't worry about the money, people will give what you need." It was a "God thang" because they did just that.

This is definitely true of my culture, family and friends usually bring one or both food and monetary donations during home goings.

I've known more families with loved ones to pass away without proper burial insurance than those with it. There has been much improvement within the last decade with the education offered to perspective clients in this area.

We have better employment, a better since of financial planning and realize the burden this causes when a loved one passes and we are not prepared. The first four people that came to see me collectively brought me one third of what was needed. The following day people came with more donations. The Tuesday before the viewing one of my siblings called me and asked me if I had enough money to bury my husband. I was transparent, all pride had gone and I truthfully told him what I needed. He told me not to worry he and his wife would take care of the balance. The funeral home was expecting the balance that Thursday before the viewing he gave it to me Wednesday.

As mentioned before we do not preplan for various economic reasons. The weight of burial can become so heavy there is no time to mourn. There can be such a financial burden on the surviving mate that crying or mourning is placed on the fence until the business is handled. Making final arrangements, contacting family and friends, preparing or giving input for the printed program, there is so much to do before the final good-bye or home going service.

In our sixth year of marriage, Ted was disabled from a sizeable tumor known in the medical field as a "Hemangioblastoma." This was his second episode, the first was before we were married but the surgery and hospital stay was brief and there was no lengthy rehabilitation period. The doctor said it was possible for this type of tumor to reoccur, that was in 1991.

The first was cerebellar. Cerebellar hemangioblastomas may cause difficulty with gait (ataxia), co-ordination or nystagmus (oscillation of the eyes on lateral gaze toward the side of the tumor). His symptoms were vomiting and dizziness brought on by the room appearing to spin.

They found one large and five small tumors in the first surgery. The surgeon said when they opened him up the tumors popped out from the pressure. If he had walked around just two-weeks more his head would have exploded from the inside out.

These symptoms were reoccurring for months and he was in and out of emergency rooms because he lacked any kind of medical benefits or insurance. With that he was treated for inner ear infection, sinusitis and a couple more diagnosis.

That is what the emergency room is for to treat the symptoms and patch you up until you can see your regular physician. When the symptoms began in February 1991, I would take him to emergency at least once or twice a week, sometimes sitting 8-12 hours in the waiting room, leaving in just enough time to take him home and then go home, shower and go to work.

During this time Ted had broken up with his girlfriend, I was going through a nerve-racking divorce and she and his mom thought he was suffering from "love pains." But I often wondered did not the symptoms make them feel it could be something more serious, especially since the occurrences became more frequent with more intensity and he was losing weight... maybe not. Ted and I were friends for twelve years. We met in a local Gospel Music Workshop and both had our own workshops, his for adults and mine targeted youth. Being freshly divorced and taking him (a single man) back and forth to the hospital caused gossip but I knew my motives were to help.

It is no secret or surprise how busy the mouths of unhappy, gossipy women in church can be. Had to keep reminding myself of Proverbs 18:21, "Death and life [are] in the **power** of the **tongue**: and they that love it shall eat the fruit thereof." My flesh wanted to retaliate with an ole' fashion beat down but never did I give in.

I do not regret helping or enduring the gossip because his doctor told me my persistence saved his life. It was during this time we began to see each other differently as more than friends. We both believe it was a match made divinely in heaven especially since I was not looking to be married ever again. I enjoyed our friendship because he helped keep me grounded. Nothing like a wounded sista' looking for revenge it can be a dangerous thing.

Chapter 2
ROUND TWO

We married July 6, 1996, and the second occurrence with tumors was in May 2003. It was the largest his physicians had ever seen and no textbook information was available as how to remove it surgically. The tumor entwines and feeds off the blood vessels and can cause extensive blood loss during surgery. The tumor looked like an alien was attached to his spine on the MRI it wrapped around and bored into his spine. The neurosurgeon's prognosis was complete paralysis and or loss of life. Ted opted to have the surgery; he believed God would work a miracle.

We had just physically moved to Long Beach, California the night before his scheduled surgery. When the diagnosis was confirmed we had less than 30 days to try and find a suitable place preferably with no stairs. At this time we lived in an apartment with three flights of stairs. The best we could do was a place near my god son with 15 steps. This was important because we believed God for a miracle and yet did not know what condition he would come home in (just being realistic).

The scheduled six-hour surgery progressed into eleven hours. He was admitted at 6:00 a.m. and the surgery began around 2:00 p.m. A hospital policy that upset us both was he had to go to pre-op alone. We discovered this when the orderly came to take him up with the other patients. I remember the statement the orderly made, "Kiss your loved ones good bye, no one else beyond this point." It sounded so final and eerie to say the least. We thought we would be together until he was ready for surgery. We held each other in the middle of the hallway sobbing. This was not what we expected. I sat in the waiting room downstairs with 50 or so other people. Trying to be strong was no use, as I cried profusely. People glaring at me did not bother nor shame me, I was beyond being embarrassed. How would I know if the surgery was successful or when it was over? This was my concern.

The receptionist stated I would be called over the PA system when the surgery was complete. After about 2.5 hours the suspense was too stressful so I decided to go home while I was emotionally able to drive. Not knowing my way around Long Beach, I definitely did not want to be looking for my place of residence in the dark. We got lost when we moved in the night before.

Aimlessly I made a few pit stops, to the Post Office, and Kaiser Pharmacy in Inglewood. As I walked to the service window with red, watery eyes from crying, the clerks in each location knew me and inquired to my distress. At each stop the clerks said, "He will be alright, God will take care of him." Same encouraging words came from an elderly woman in the waiting room at Kaiser. Did not I know this? What was wrong with me and my faith? I called my mom and she suggested I pull over and have a good cry before I wrap my car around a pole...I did and it helped. Traveling home from Kaiser Sunset by way of the 101, 110, 405 and 710 freeways, to 4th Street in Long beach was none eventful.

Upon my return home I called our families and our pastors. After the eighth hour my pastor called and said Ted's spirit was pulling on his spirit and he was going to the hospital. The only information received when I called was, "He is not out of surgery yet." I did not know what floor or room the surgery was taking place. My Pastor offered to provide me transportation but I wanted someone else to tell me (play by play) before I saw him. Yes, I was a wimp for a moment ... AND WHAT?

Communicating with me by cell phone the Spirit of God led my Pastor right to Ted as they were wheeling him from surgery into recovery. After giving consent for the doctors to give him information he passed it on to me. I remember him asking me, "Do you want the good news or the bad news first?" I was numb, it did not matter. The doctors said his left arm would probably be paralyzed and that his blood pressure was dangerously elevated. "Did he have a history of high blood pressure?" "No, he did not," I replied.

His face was badly swollen because he laid face down for over eleven hours of surgery. Pastor prayed covering him from head to toe declaring healing over his entire body. The prognosis as I mentioned earlier were he would be quadriplegic (totally paralyzed), then he was upgraded to paraplegic being paralyzed from the waist down and then there was God's prognosis, (stay with me). After getting his blood pressure and pain meds stabilized (he was receiving a morphine drip and patch at the same time causing him to be semi-comatose). The surgery could possibly have taken his life but the mistake with medications almost did.

While recovering in intensive care patients sit on a cardiac chair for so many hours a day of which he constantly complained of pain on his buttocks, mind you the surgery was on the back of his neck and the upper portion of the back. He had a five inch scar we called "the life line." After a few days of this I find that a nurse in the hospital placed him in a leather cardiac chair without a sheet between his bottom and the chair. His skin stuck to the chair and when the lift team picked him up to place him back in the bed it ripped the skin off of his buttocks. This still gives me chills and turns my stomach as I write about it. Thus we now have the beginning of a decubadus ulcer which became dangerously infected and could result in death if the infection spread to the blood or the bone.

A fairly new treatment using a wound-vacuum was used to aspirate the infection and speed up the healing process. A small tube was place in the wound and the machine vacuumed out infection which induced healing. The event caused by the chair occurred on the first Friday (five days after his surgery) but was not discovered until the following Monday. You already know what I did, went jungle crazy on them with my saved self.

After a one-month stay in the hospital Ted was discharged and sent to a skilled nursing facility and there for three months he was given extensive physical and occupational therapy. They had to teach him to walk, feed, dress, bathe and care for himself.

It was arduous work having to do this with a decubadus ulcer on his bottom which was uncomfortable and painful. The wound-vacuum was still attached and added to the discomfort.

Twice a day therapist worked to help him regain his mobility beginning with basic sitting, standing, taking steps, walking, and regaining the use of his hands and arms to promote the ability for him dressing and feeding his self (all reminding me how babies develop).

The physical therapy was grueling. It was difficult seeing my once healthy, robust husband progress feebly from bed, to wheel chair to walker. He lost over 50 pounds during this process. He was so thin and the thought of him suffering was agonizing and overwhelming for me. When he returned home (three days before Thanksgiving) I fattened him up with some good wholesome cooking.

The physical therapy continued and Ted was about 90% his old self. We began to enjoy life even more because it was a reality for us that the conditions of life can change, be shortened, or halted at any given time. It was a lesson for us not taking the *little things* we do on a daily basis for granted. Although, the doctor never released him to drive, we took cruises, went to the movies, walked on the beach and were very active in our church serving as executive pastors. Our love continued to grow and although we were home together twenty-four seven, we never grew tired of being together. It was an amazing relationship.

We did not have intense fellowships (arguments) because for me, I had been there and done that and he was not a fan of arguing. After two failed marriages both due to my former spouse' infidelity and other stupid stuff, I did not have the patience to play games or squabble.

Often I have stated our relationship was what most dreamed of having. Not bragging but excited to know there was such a thing as mutual love and faithfulness in a relationship. There are a few good men living on earth after all they all did not come from Mars. How many women can honestly say without apprehension they have known and experienced real true love? I know from experience how it is to be in a marriage of distrust wondering where your mate is and who may be with him.

There is no joy surreptitiously desiring qualities in a person you know will never be, pretending to be happy when much more is being desired. Many a spouse finds themselves hanging on to one-sided relationships, giving their all and hoping for a *little* something in return.

Being played the fool is no fun. In the previous marriage everyone *seemed to know our business mainly due to my ex-husband's* uncontrollable flesh problem and lack of respect and discretion. After two previously failed marriages I was done. It was my time and my turn to return the favor of hurt. But praise God, He had something different in mind and sent me a Boaz and I reluctantly tried one more time. They say the third time is a charm and it was that for me. But my advice is to get it right the first time around. Divorce affects more than the couple, your children, families, church family and friends can all be affected. Allow God to send you who He has for you. I was blessed not to have just a second but to have a third chance.

Chapter 3
ROUND THREE

We never had children together but I had three from my previous marriages and he discovered in 2006, (ten years into our marriage) he had a daughter 23 years old. They met on mutual grounds at our church and from that point spent time catching up on years lost and looking forward to celebrating years to come. In March 2007, she birthed twin boys. Not only did he have a child but he had three grandchildren (to my one). She has a six year old handsome son we call "Q."

However in May, 2007, before our last cruise together Ted became symptomatic again. As his condition slowly worsened I especially did not feel comfortable trying to go on excursions away from the cruise ship. His gait was off and he was experiencing numbness in both hands. While on the cruise, he had difficulty cutting his meat and the warm climate in the ports (we cruised the Mexican Rivera) seemed to cause him great discomfort so we spent most of the last three days of the cruise aboard the ship. We busied ourselves with activities he was comfortable with. I did not want him to feel as though he was spoiling things for us. A greater concern was being able to finish the cruise with him walking off the ship.

When we returned we made an emergency appointment for a MRI (he was scheduled for one in June) and discovered there were two small tumors each about the size of a quarter, one on the upper and one on the lower spine. We were devastated. Up to this point his walking was seriously affected and weight loss was rapid even though he had what seemed to be a healthy appetite. The neurologist immediately scheduled him for a new chemotherapy, called Avastin that actually had no real side effects. It was though water was pumping through his veins.

There were also 25 sessions of radiation therapy scheduled (five days a week for five consecutive weeks). The radiation treatments ceased mid treatment because it was evident it was not helping and he began experiencing intense side-effects. If the treatment had worked, he would have made medical history. The neurosurgeon said Avastin had not been used for the treatment of this type tumor.

We lived up one flight of stairs, 15 steps and our neighbors helped me navigate him up and down the stairs for about two weeks. My eldest son tried to take family leave from his job but could not because Ted was not his biological parent. Instead, he drove and helped me transport Ted two days a week on his days off. At this point Ted had to be assisted into and out of the car into a wheel chair. During the radiation treatment, he began experiencing infections and elevated blood sugar resulting from the high dosage of steroids.

Following the advice of the radiologist we went to emergency and found his blood sugar was over 400, and he had a form of thrash a white, cottage cheese looking infection in his mouth and down his throat. He was admitted and never returned home again.

In the emergency room Ted told me emphatically while waiting he could not make it up the stairs again in his condition. He did not want to come home if he was going to have to walk up the stairs. The stairs were a great concern because it took almost 20 minutes to get him up or down. When admitted he was very frail, had lost his color and the infection affected his voice causing him to talk a little above a whisper. No longer able to feed his self or use the phone because his hands were almost completely paralyzed he had the nurses and visitors call me and hold the phone to his ear so we could talk. While in this condition he did not want to come home. Trying to remember (you know how you put things way in the back of your mind) I believe this is the point I began to waiver in my faith and fall apart because the prognosis was not good. Can I be honest? What I saw on a daily basis sometimes caused me to forget to hold tighter to my faith. At times I found myself being influenced by the physician's and specialist reports when I should have believed the report of the Lord.

The Word Says:

*1 Peter 2:24; "Who **his** own self bare our sins in **his** own body on the tree that we, being dead to sins, should live unto righteousness: by whose **stripes** ye were healed."*

*Psalm 107:20; He **sent his word**, and **healed** them, and delivered [them] from their destructions.*

We had been through this twice before and God raised him up. God was still God...wasn't He? I knew this, I knew and believed God's Word and yet found myself sometimes consumed with what the physicians were saying. Walking by sight and not as I should by faith.

The hospital was a good place for him to be because the staff was trained and would monitor his intake of food, liquids, and blood sugar, and weight loss, give supplements and know when and what treatment was needed. Ted began to improve. His voice returned for about a week, he was more alert and his skin seemed healthier. He had a positive attitude and I had my spiritual facade together. Had to be prayed up and down because if I seemed worried he would worry and if I seemed tired he would feel bad about me making the drive. Superwoman is who I was and had to be.

One of the nurses at the skilled nursing facility employed by Kaiser talked to me about taking care of myself. She had come into the room to check on Ted and asked if she could talk to me in her office (I probably looked as tired as I was feeling like a beat up over bleached dish rag). She explained that from her many years of experience when the caregiver neglects their own needs, they usually give out long before the person who is convalescing. Taking her advice my visits reduced to every other day.

But there was a plan in place to make sure Ted was not neglected. He had so many visitors in and out day and night the nurses thought he was pastor of a church. Members of our church, friends and family visited on the days I did not.

My greatest concern was his comfort, being monitored properly and just receiving the care he needed.

Even though it was a greater drive for me at Ted's request he was placed in the same skilled nursing facility he was in four years prior, twenty six miles one way from home.

The car needed an oil change and while leaving from the service department at Cerritos Nissan I received a call from Ted's physician as I pulled off the parking lot. He asked me if I had considered Hospice. Ignorant of what "Hospice" was I inquired thinking it was a place and not a preparation. Hospice is when one is sent home or to a facility to prepare to die. This was the physician's exact words.

Of course, you guessed it, I lost it! Crying and sobbing profusely I had to pull over to the curb and try and gather myself. Did I mention I was given this news while driving?

My experience with some medical professionals who work in a particular field for an extended period of time is they seem to forget about having a "bed side manner." They see dying and death so often they become immune to its effects on others. You cannot really get angry about that because they need some kind of mental technique to be able to keep their sanity. I thank God I was not on the freeway because I was a Holy Ghost mess. These encounters always seem to happen when no one else was around.

In times of panic or anguish we so easily forget about our greatest help...God. We think if our pastor, children, brother, aunt, uncle, momma, daddy, best friend, if anybody was with us we could process the news better. Once we stop slobbering and slinging spit we remember...God is here. Then (after the fact) we get deep and start saying in our spirit, Psalm 46:1 *"God [is] our refuge and strength, a very **present help** in trouble."*

Psalm 27:1 *"The LORD [is]* **my light** *and* **my salvation***; whom shall I fear? the LORD [is] the strength of* **my** *life; of whom shall I be afraid?"*

God was probably saying, "Girl Please. Now you want to remember me?" A little levity, it's alright to laugh, especially when the joke is on me. Allow me to continue with a more serious attitude. The next day Ted and I discussed his physician's plans and he was quite upset because they were giving up on him so easily. He made a statement to the doctor, "I would like to think my life was worth more than what you are willing to put into it." What we did not know at this time was the tumors were cancerous and aggressively growing and would soon affect his upper respiratory, making breathing difficult. Yes, I know, God was still a healer especially if He raised the dead surely He could manifest a miraculous healing. He did it before, remember?

Before he was admitted Ted was given the option of surgery. He opted not to have surgery because the odds were one of four patients were paralyzed and he did not want to go through the intense rehabilitation again or not have the quality of life predicted by the surgeon. I recall him saying, "I am going to believe God will work another miracle, but I do not want surgery."

Thinking in retrospect his attitude this time was if he knew something I did not. He even asked me if I would be angry if he chose not to have the surgery. How could I be? I wanted what he wanted but I did want him to live. But the choice was his to make. None of the treatment worked and his deterioration was progressive. He went from smiling when I entered his room to not eating, to having a feeding tube and to a state of no response. I played worship music so his spirit could be ministered to and refused to give up hope. From his waste up he looked well. It was important to me that I honored him in this manner. His face was full; his hair neatly cut and face closely shaved. Most of the weight loss seemed to be from his hips down. Atrophy was setting in his legs which were very thin, and there was very little muscle.

I stopped allowing doubt to creep into my mind and began reinforcing myself with the Word. No matter what was said, no matter what they showed me, no matter how things looked I knew I must believe God and stand on His Word.

I remembered Jude 20: *But you, dear friends, build yourselves up in your most holy faith and pray in the Holy Spirit.* We build ourselves up in the faith by the study of God's Word.

I mentioned earlier that we must make daily deposits of the Word of God in our spirit so when times such as these come we can withdraw. It is difficult to trust in someone we do not know and do not have true relationship with. So it is with trusting God when we don't know Him; but the better we know Him, the more we can trust Him. We pray in the Holy Spirit: by asking the Holy Spirit to direct our prayers, and when we groan (Romans 8:26-27), and by praying in unknown tongues (1 Cor. 14:2).

Ted was a very stylish person who took pride in his appearance. He made costume jewelry using Austrian crystal which was a hit with the sistas' in church. For men he made button covers, tie pins and brooches. When we first met, he often mentioned how he went to the movies in a suit and tie. You must realize during this time we were both in a liberated ministry which taught and practiced Bible doctrine and not man-made principals. I realized someone had to change and it was not going to be me. It felt real good in the winter to be able to wear pants and keep my legs warm.

Being creative and thoughtful in a crafty way one of his Christmas gifts were a pair of jeans. From that time on he began dressing a bit more relaxed and casual when any event called for it. He loved me and I him and he did not want to disappoint me and he wanted to change. Change is not always easy coming from the bondage of stringent religious rules and traditions but he learned well.

As I share a little about his character and personality you can understand better the kind of man he was. At 13 he was a licensed minister, choir director, songwriter, preacher, teacher and so much more. He lifted weights for years and had a physique like "Popeye the Sailor." Chest so robust he always had difficulty purchasing dress shirts and suits. A handsome, stylish dresser, thoughtful, caring and I had it all and a bag of chips.

We made a handsome couple. We really enjoyed being together. He helped with laundry and other chores men would call "a woman's work." He did everything but cook and that was cool with me because I never liked house work but enjoyed baking and cooking.

Ted spoiled me big time. This was the first and only man that opened doors for me and pulled the chair out in restaurants. When we first started hanging out I would jump out the door as soon as the car stopped. Hey! I was not use to a polite man. I was comfortably independent but you better believe I was a quick learner.

As I yet believed God for a miracle when I returned home one night after my regular visit I sat at the computer and began putting a home going program together. This was not something I wanted to do because I was yet looking for a miracle. But my spirit would not let me rest until I did. My granddaughter Ashley was with me and she asked me was he going to die. I was honest, (she was 15) and told her I do not know what God has in store but I am being lead to do this. She sat with me and made some suggestions. When he passed away, I thoroughly understood the events of this night.

In the skilled nursing facility there were "saved" nurses tending to him on every shift. They continued the worship music day and night. They would call me and hold the phone so we could talk. Even when he was nonresponsive he could hear the music because sometimes tears would roll down his face as the music ministered to his spirit.

Whenever I began walking by sight and not by faith I would get a check in my spirit and continued to believe God for the manifestation of his healing. When he became nonresponsive I talked close to and directly in his ear and told him, "I love you and I miss you and still

29

believing God." Sometimes he would smile. I anointed him with oil and would pray in the spirit over him. Out of those visiting him not all were released to pray for him because not all people know that there are different prayers for our varied needs. Some pray foolishly and that he did not need. Despite my moments of frailty there was never a time I doubted God's ability to make him whole.

Chapter 4
A FAITH CHALLENGE

During his last battle I found there was a lot of denial (not a loss of hope so much) but a lot of denial on my part. I yet believed God could work another miracle for him, believing his condition could reverse. There is nothing too hard for God. That is what Jeremiah 32:17 says: *"Ah, Sovereign Lord, you have made the heavens and the earth by your great power and outstretched arm. Nothing is too hard for you."* People all over, from coast to coast were interceding for his recovery. One of the most difficult strengths to muster up was seeing in the natural and yet believing (undoubtedly) in the spiritual as the negative reports rolled in. It is very important that we have spiritually mature people around during these times. They help us stay focused and remain rooted and grounded and they will hold our arms up like Aaron and Hur did for Moses when we grow tired.

A hospice team was sent to persuade me to accept what they saw as inevitable as I was trying to see Jesus in it all. My husband declined from talking and eating to not recognizing or responding to me or anyone else. After 4-weeks in the skilled nursing facility, he was given two-weeks to live. It was though I was living a nightmare from some horror movie. He had only celebrated his 50th birthday in January of this same year and I was seven years his senior. He could not be dying. We had too much to do, too much life left to live together, too much ministry work incomplete. The book he was writing on Praise and Worship was not complete. He had just discovered he had a daughter and only saw his grandchildren once and could not hold them because his hands could not support their weight. Terminal illness, not the man of my dreams! Not my Boaz! "God, what is going on here?" I screamed silently.

I slapped myself upside the head and came to my senses realizing that God is sovereign. He can do and does what He wants when He wants and how He wants to. No matter how astute we are, or how prayed up we think we are, or how close our daily walk with God is, we will never know everything. God is not going to reveal everything to us. This is when our trust and faith has to ignite. After I busted up my own pity party and began finding ways to cope and keep my sanity, God began revealing himself to me. Not realizing it at the time. I was going to need my strength to deal with some ignorant "church folk" and be able to have integrity doing it. Because we are saved, we do not forget how to do things we should not do, we just choose not to do them and I was being challenged.

My flesh wanted to give them a tongue thrashing their ears had never heard. God's choicest vessels (they would have you to think), some sanctified, Holy Ghost filled, people of God told me: "You did not pray earnestly enough," "Ted should not have died," "Ted must have really pissed God off," "Why aren't you going to tell his mother, she needs to know?" His mother was in the advanced stages of Alzheimer in a skilled nursing facility and had a heart condition. The physicians asked us not to tell her because she would not remember it and it was possible she would not process it in a healthy manner. Some of the saints threatened to go and tell her anyway. They were so rude and obnoxious.

One dear saint came to the viewing and began to boisterously address me about not telling his mom. Knowing how inconsiderate people can be my daughter and a couple of friends were assigned to protect me from the foolish. Ted's brother (who passed away 22 months after him from liver disease) had to put a hold on his mom's visitation for over a month. They continued calling me never asking how I was doing but wanting to know if his mother had been told. They reminded me of venomous snakes. They talked as if they had purchased a "god" license at a Sear's department store sale. After things quieted down some, I requested they not call me again and most have not gone to visit his mom because they feel it is too far to travel. The facility that is caring for his mom is 35 miles from Long Beach, California.
These are saints that have known her and have been friends for over 40 years. Go figure.

Shiela Y. Harris

The Thursday before Ted's passing my eldest son accompanied me to visit him. The Holy Spirit instructed me to do the following. I leaned over and kissed him and whispered, "If it is time for you to go, do not worry about me, I will be alright. You do not have to hold on because of me. I love you." I heard crying and sobbing and turned around to see my eldest son bawling.

I am trying to be strong and he is bawling. He said he just could not take it. My children and family really loved Ted because of how he loved and treated me. Ted had a prophetic mantle on his life and I had to be strong so he would believe I would be alright.

While he was coherent in the hospital and the skilled nursing facility he was prophesying and encouraging the staff and other patients. But all who knew him also knew that was Ted's life once he truly accepted that mantle. He was not only a preacher and teacher but a true prophet of God.

That same night I prayed and talked to God. It was not that I couldn't but I did not want to go through this again nor did I want Ted to go through it again. My prayer was, *"Father God in heaven, I love you and I thank you for your Grace and your Mercy. I pray your perfect will be done in Ted's life and mine. I believe and stand on the Word you've inspired and spoken. But if he is not going to get well please do not allow him to lie in the state he is in now and suffer. Father, please forgive me for my weak moments because I trust you in every aspect of our lives. I need your strength to endure whatever lies ahead for us. And God, whatever you decide to do in our lives I will accept, in Jesus name. Amen."*

Ted passed away two days later on a Saturday morning, September 8, 2007, at 7:05 a.m. The tumors were aggressive and grew most on the part of the brain that controls respiratory function. I was at home preparing for my daily visit when the call came.

The doctor said he did not suffer he just slept away. Imagine this: He went to sleep and woke up in the presence of God. Oh Glory!

33

Numb and unresponsive to the call with disbelief is what I remember. It has been one year and two months and some days are more difficult than others.

It is important to take it one day at a time. When you love someone so much as we loved one another you cannot help missing their presence as you remember, reflecting on the good times. My pastor made a statement to me a few months after his demise.

He said, "You do not have to be sad because Ted surely is not sad. He is in heaven in the presence of God and would not come back if he could." This helped me tremendously because the pain of grief became less and the happiness of good memories became more.

But let's park here for a moment. What was God up to? Ted was a miracle, a walking testimony from his last occurrence and it was prophesied to him (by a credible prophet) he would never have to go through that type of sickness again. Honestly, I was never angry with God, but I did want to understand why.

Yes, God can do what He wants, when He wants and how He wants to but understanding was what I needed and it was not happening. I thought I could cope better if I understood why. But in all actuality I also knew we are not going to know or understand everything God does or allows.

For a while it seemed as though this had not happened, that I was having a dream and soon I would awaken to reality. It was approximately one year after his passing before I truly released him and really accepted Ted was gone.

Grief is an unpredictable experience even for Christians. No one can say how we will grieve or how we will go through the process. One thing is certain we must go through the process.
Many churches are not prepared to professionally help their members go through and survive the grieving process in a healthy manner and can often give useless and unhealthy advice.

This is a time I really appreciated my Senior Pastor honestly confessing our ministry was not equipped to counsel in the area of grief and for me to take advantage of whatever was available. He was also closely connected to Ted and I, we had ministry history together and it would have been difficult.

This book came about because my pastor told me to take notes, keep a journal and hold on to the information accessed through group meetings because ministry was going to birth from this. He spiritually went through this process with me at the threshold of my emotions and recognized that part of the purpose was to birth a much needed ministry for bereavement. As awful as I felt at times he saw supernatural strength and anointing on me. Now I am sure some are reading this and thinking, "Why would anyone want to journal or take notations of such and emotional and painful event and then read and relive it?"

To understand this you must understand my pastors and the anointing on their lives. I thoroughly understood if I can go through the grieving and survive this process a powerful testimony will develop that will help multitudes.

Prayer is the key to heaven and faith unlocks the door. But there will be circumstances when we will need to know how to emotionally survive a negative experience. We know about prayer and believe strongly in its power but somehow, no matter how strong we think we are death can cause vulnerability and a loss of reality. You know God exists but there are times it seems you are spiritually disconnected. People, family and friends can help but it may take professional help to understand the various emotions a loss through death can waken. There were a myriad of emotions and what makes it tangible and incomprehensible at the same time is to experience your own personal loss.

To wake up one day happily and blissfully married, and go to sleep that night a widow. Our lives can change in an instant and we do not think much about this probability until it actually happens. Losing my husband felt as though I had lost a limb in an unsuccessful surgery with the wound still exposed. My God! It is important to me that you feel and understand the anguish.

I recalled a book written by the well-known Bishop, T.D. Jakes (cannot remember the title) in which he described his feelings or emotions through his mother's illness and death. A great orator, author, and pastor of thousands sharing how tedious it was to care for her and how she digressed from a vibrant woman into sickness and then death. I appreciated his honesty about his emotions and how sometimes it was a struggle for him to preach and feed his flock. He was grieving, and he had to go through the process before he could heal. I do not recall any great religious heroics but I do recall a great man humanly dealing with the pain a loss through death can cause. I've often wonder if he was able to properly grieve the loss.

Chapter 5
HEALTHY GRIEVING

One of the greatest survival tools aside from relationship with God was grief counseling. My Pastor recommended me availing myself to whatever help I needed. He and his wife were a great support. They called every day for about two months. Sometimes I was cool and sometimes I was a basket case. He prayed, encouraged me and let me know they were there for me no matter what time day or night. He always inquired about my health (sleeping and eating habits … I was losing weight). Ministry leaders must be careful who they "bleed" to but one thing I could not do and probably should have was called people late at night that offered and availed themselves. Each time I would attempt to dial a number I would hang up because I felt bad about waking them out of their sleep. In the early stages my medical plan provided a 24-hour number of trained staff tending the phones. Yes, and I used that puppy a few times.

Soon I realized grief is a process that we all will go through. Most of us are not prepared and certainly would rather by pass it if we could. Psalm 91:1; *"Those who live in the shelter of the Most High will find rest in the shadow of the Almighty."* No matter how great the agony there is a place where you and I can live in Jesus Christ, a place of safety, peace, and joy (Chuck Smith Commentary). I reached my load bearing weight. Sleepless nights, periods of uncontrollable crying, despair and loneliness all while strongly knowing, having relationship with and trusting God. The inability of recognizing or knowing what was normal for a time such as this was due to no former experience to measure my emotions by.

The grief counseling was not in a religious setting but neither was it atheistic. Nowadays, we must be "politically correct" in public settings respecting everyone's beliefs. To do this, society removes God from the equation. During this process God set me up. I went into my first session wounded and came out a nurturer.

In the first session I realized that what I was experiencing was very normal, I was not losing my mind after all. I set thinking, "Whew, thank you Jesus!" The facilitators make sure we are in a safe haven type of environment. No one is to discuss what goes on nor are we to tell others in the session how to cope. We introduce ourselves, tell who or what we lost, the date and cause of death if we are comfortable with that. As we discussed our emotions a man asked me (my loss was the most recent – a little over a month) how was I coping so well, if they only knew. I explained to the group that the only way I could explain was to share my greatest support and would have to mention "God." They all agreed and none would be offended. The Holy Spirit began to use me in an intellectual way as I began to tell them of my Faith and belief and because of it, God is sustaining me. Even though it was a very difficult time for me I believed God would and was carrying me through.

Not having experienced the loss of a mate I needed to know what was a normal healthy way of grieving and what was detrimental. Let's pause here again. For the record, <u>I never felt suicidal</u>. Through all my crying and sleepless nights I realized the grieving process can open the door for the enemy, especially the door to our mind. I remembered **Isaiah 26:3** *"Thou wilt keep [him] in **perfect peace**, [whose] mind [is] stayed [on thee]: because he trusteth in thee."* You will keep him in perfect peace: What a promise! Perfect peace! God promises that we can have perfect peace, and even be kept in a place of perfect peace. (David Guzik Commentary) I was tired and I wanted and needed peace. I was tired of the up this hour down the next.

In Hebrew, the term **perfect peace** is actually *shalom shalom*. This shows how in Hebrew, repetition communicates intensity. It isn't just *shalom*; it is *shalom shalom*, **perfect peace**.

It is astonishing that we can have this **perfect peace**, but for some it is fleeting and they are never kept there. Others can be kept **in peace**, but it is not a **perfect peace**, it is the peace of the wicked, the peace of spiritual sleep and ultimate destruction. But there is a **perfect peace** that the LORD will **keep** us in.

Whose mind is stayed on you: This is the place of **perfect peace**, and the source of it. When we keep our minds stayed – settled upon, established upon - the Lord Himself, then we can be kept in this perfect peace. (David Guzik Commentary)

Another scripture quickened in my spirit, *"The thief cometh not, but for to steal, and to kill, and to destroy: I am come that they might have* ***life****, and that they might have [it]* ***more abundantly****, "* John 10:10. God had me realize through all of this, I had to guard my mind. Grief opens the door to depression, which opens the door to all sorts of demonic attacks in our mind and body.

Let's pause again for a moment. This may seem harsh but true. No matter what we go through, if we meditate on it day and night we lose sight of Christ and the **"it"** becomes our god. Episodes of our lives can sometimes be totally and unequivocally devastating. Personally I am acquainted with a woman who lost two adult children within one month of the other. I have three adult children and cannot even begin to imagine this. A parishioner in our ministry lost two relatives (twin sister and sister-in-law) within six-months of each other. Ted's Brother Frankie passed away 22 months after him from the rejection of his second liver transplants. He left his wife, two children in the home and other children he fathered over the years. He married in the same month and year of Ted and me, three weeks from our date July 21, 1996. Frankie accepted Christ two weeks before he passed. He was not sure if he had done so in his life. He would joke saying he and Teddy would play checkers in heaven. Can you even imagine what his wife is experiencing with two young children?

It is so important for the Believer to be knowledgeable of the Word because it is through the Word we receive direction for our lives even in the midst of storms.

As we compare weather storms with the storms of our lives it makes since. The eye of the storm is a region of mostly calm weather found at the center of strong tropical cyclones.

In all storms, however, the eye is the location of the storm's minimum barometric pressure: the area where the atmospheric pressure at sea level is the lowest. (Wikipedia Online Encyclopedia)

Our summation can be the safest place in a crisis is in the eye of its storm. This is God. He is the safe place in the midst of our storms. The safe place when the storms of our lives are raging we can be reassured that God is with us. Sometimes as we ride out the storm and strong winds of life blow hurricane strength and our way seems dark and blurry but we are never alone and will be victorious if we faint not.

Isaiah says it so eloquently in 40:31; *"But they that wait upon the LORD shall renew [their] strength; they shall mount up with wings as eagles; they shall run, and not be weary; [and] they shall walk, and not faint."*

Ephesians 3:13; *"Wherefore I desire that ye faint not at my tribulations for you, which is your glory."*

Therefore I ask that you do not lose heart: Though under arrest for the sake of the gospel, Paul asks his readers to not **lose heart**. Paul didn't want them to be discouraged for *his* sake, because Paul was still being used in the service of God's eternal plan.

My tribulations for you: Paul wrote the Letter to the Ephesians from prison. Paul was being used, and probably in greater way than he ever imagined. This Roman imprisonment produced the letters of Ephesians, Colossians, Philippians and Philemon. They all certainly have a place in God's eternal plan.

Which is your glory: In the same manner, each of us has a place in the service of God's eternal plan. Knowing this and working towards it is a great guard against losing heart in the midst of tribulation. (David Guzik Commentary)

After the dismissal of my first grief counseling session five people came to me crying and confessing their weaknesses and some with substance abuse dependency such as, alcohol binging, and so forth.

They wanted to have whatever coping-mechanism it was I had so they too could survive. Discretely, more as a testimony I introduced Jesus Christ to them and told them having Him in my life and accepting Him as my Savior assures me He is carrying me through and would carry them through without any type of dependency on substance and its abuse.

I had to be careful because they could band me from the sessions if I broke the rules and I was still inside the conference room. But I believe I was able to complete the assignment God sent me in there to do. What a Holy Ghost setup.

What happened in there? God set me up. He had me to realize He was always with me. Angels were with me. The Holy Spirit was with me. In the midst of my pain and reaching out for professional help I was sent on a mission. One of which I had to lay aside my needs and recognize I had the one thing that the others did not and that was Jesus Christ as Savior of my life.

I did receive a lot of help on a professional level in the next five sessions. If we can understand the process of grieving and its emotional affect as well as what to expect we can go through, survive it and still have a yet praise.

Chapter 6
WHAT IS GRIEF?

The definition of grief includes: emotions and sensations that accompany the loss of someone or something dear to you. The English word comes from the Old French *grève*, meaning a heavy burden. This makes sense when you consider with some people grief overwhelmingly weighs them down with feelings of sorrow and other out-of-control emotions that can have both psychological and physical effects.

Losing someone or something you love is very painful — and it's something that almost everyone will experience at some point in their lives. Loss that goes unacknowledged or unattended can result in disability. But grief that is expressed and experienced has a potential for healing that eventually can strengthen and enrich life. There is no right or wrong way to grieve — but there are ways to make your grieving more complete and more positive. (HelpGuide.org)

The grief process is being able to retell the story of loss, expressing the hurt and pain, accepting that the loved one is gone, though never forgotten and going on with life's activities. In most cases people can make this transition within a year of monthly group sessions and returning to a support group occasionally if there is an anniversary or another loss to receive the support necessary to get through this time. My choice was to write this book and use the material in group settings to help others through the process.

People grieve over many things. We grieve over loss of life, relationships, loss of employment, our home and even pets. Reminded of the loss of my dad at the age of 15, I thought that was difficult. He was ill for a long time suffering from complications of diabetes symptoms and some form of cancer.

I was the only girl and horribly spoiled by my dad. But the love I had for my dad is different than the love I have for my husband and will be different considering most cases depending on the relationship we have for those we love and lose through death.

At the onset of writing this book I reflected on some of the emotions I experienced. Having eleven years of living in the home with someone twenty-four seven, to being alone in the home twenty-four seven. Having someone to talk about everything with to listening to the voices on the radio, television or the people I talked with over the telephone. Having the opportunity to travel everywhere with your confidant and companion, to driving and attending events alone. Experiencing intimacy (not just sexually) and loving being around my mate to surviving on recalled memories. This was my experience after his death because for me, as long as he was alive I had hope in having these things again. In the course of a day, I lost everything we had together as husband and wife, as best friends, as my ministry partner, movie going, cruise traveling, shopping partner.

Around the first six months after my husband's death the Holy Spirit ministered to me. It is something I believe many of us forget during times of bereavement. Not because we want to but sometimes the pain of the loss distracts us so much we fail to see God at these moments of our lives. It was on a day I was bawling, not wanting to get out of bed, no appetite just an emotional wreck, during one of my "melt-downs." As I was crying out to God to keep my mind, to help me shake the emotional roller coaster, the Spirit of God ministered to me. He said, "You can never <u>love</u> anyone or anything more than you <u>love</u> me." "Whoa…," that was heavy.

In all actuality, I forgot God gives us life and He can take life. All I thought about was my loss, my pain, my hurt. He gives us our mates (well some of us find our own mates), children, family, friends and He can receive them unto himself.

Life is like a property lease that has no ending date. For the Saved, a lease runs out on earth but continues for eternity in heaven but we never know the date of transition…only God knows.

It was from this point that change began to happen. It was like falling face down in the mud and wallowing in it and then getting up, getting cleaned up and being careful to maneuver around he puddles. I will never forget that rhema Word from God.

There is so much to do when a loved one passes. If you do not have anyone to handle the major affairs and you are the executor left to do the planning it can be a heavy load. I recommend pre-planning. Have numbers on hand for facilities that offer Grief Counseling, if your church does not. This I highly recommend. If your medical plan does not offer it check your local mental health facilities, hospital, hospice, and social services.

Check with your provider to see if they offer referrals. There are various support groups such as Parents without Partners which assist people who are divorced, separated or widowed and Widowed Persons Service Program. Call the American Association of Retired Persons (AARP).

Grief can bring on a multitude of ailments or emotions and if not controlled can cause serious illness. The first symptom I remember is insomnia. Sleep is essential for our physical and mental well-being. When we are sleep-deprived, recovery from stress takes longer, and we are more likely to develop infections, high blood pressure, cardiovascular disease and diabetes. We may have problems with learning and memory, and we may be depressed and irritable, and apt to make mistakes on the job. We also have a higher risk of being in a motor vehicle crash — people with insomnia have twice as many car accidents as does the general population. (MayoClinic.com)

After 2-3 weeks of not sleeping another symptom experienced was depression. I remember episodes of uncontrollable crying, difficulty of performing normal day to day task and a feeling of hopelessness. It was at this point I was truly grateful of my relationship with God. I easily recognized that this was not the Spirit of God and if I did not get some help grief was going to destroy me.

Televisions commercials about depression screamed out at me. "Who does depression hurt…everyone…" That was me! Immediately I made an appointment with my physician.

Arriving for the appointment the check in nurse took one look at me and knew I was in some sort of trouble imagining I look a mess. Up to this point I camouflaged well, with makeup, hair neatly combed, dressed neat and clean. But on this day, eyes were red and watery, tired from not sleeping (still neat and clean). As customary they ask you "What are you seeing the doctor today for?" The bawling blurted and tears streamed. "I cannot keep going through this…I need help." I babbled with, "I cannot sleep, do not eat … my husband passed away about a month ago." She immediately assured me that I would receive the help I needed as she hurriedly summoned the doctor.

The depression signs I knew immediately. At the end of the marriage prior to Ted unknowingly I had a severe case of depression. I was able to function but physically it began to take its toll. Migraine headaches, uncontrollable blood pressure, stress and a list of other ailments. For a short while I had to take antidepressants. Yes, you better know I knew the signs!

The loss of appetite corrected itself over time. The doctor was not concerned with that symptom because I needed to lose some weight. Being aware of the lack of food consumption I made sure when I ate it was healthy and drank supplements for a while. As far as I can remember weight has always been a problem for me. Consequently I have varied sizes of clothing. Whatever happens, weight up or down there is never much concern over what to wear.

The doctor prescribed "Ambien" for sleeping and made an emergency appointment with the Grief Counseling Clinic. Yes I did! I took a sleep aid. Good Lord I was a mess! From this point on things began to settle down and improve.

Grief counseling was a small intimate setting varied by race, age, ethnicity, and sex.

We all had one thing in common, grieving a loss. Grief Counselors provided literature containing information explaining grief and its symptoms. Recognition of the signs helps us know we are not losing our minds we are just having trouble adjusting to losing someone we love dearly.

It is understandable the judgment and ridicule I may receive from being so transparent to my readers from the "deep" saints. But I am comfortable with that because regardless of what anyone thinks or says, God yet loves me, I have not lost my anointing to minister (in fact the intensity has increased), my pastors have the utmost faith in my abilities and my positioning in ministry is not affected. Meaning no disrespect, but anyone judging probably needs help and does not even realize it.

After a year or so I weaned myself off the meds and with God's help have recovered. Knowing what to expect and how to react will help me through grieving whenever there is a loss through death in the future. When I say "recover" I simply mean whenever the pain of the loss arises or I experience a melt-down it will be emotionally manageable for me.

People grieving also share some of the same emotions: Shock and Denial, Anger, Guilt, Depression, Loneliness and Hope which are also part of the cycle of grief.

Shock and Denial. One of the first reactions may be to deny the loss or to feel emotionally numb. Eventually you will be able to face the reality of your loss. Remember my comments when I received the phone call from the skilled nursing facility. This is real.

Anger. Your loss may seem unfair and you may be angry with yourself and others for not preventing the loss. But you will work through your anger. I thought about all the useless, good for nothing, men around me and was like…why are they still here? And what!

Guilt. It is not unusual to blame yourself for something you did or did not do prior to the loss. Remember you are only human, God has the final say and there are some events we cannot change, undo or control.

Depression. I recognized this from past experience and from seeing commercials, magazine advertisements and billboards regarding depression. I was like…hey…that's me! Oh my God! You may feel drained, and unable to perform even routine tasks.
Eventually, you will become yourself again. There is a difference in having an occasional emotional "melt down" and "totally loosing it."

You should watch the signs of depression because it can have such a stronghold, not eating, cannot get out of bed, stop bathing (not me), continuous uncontrollable crying spells, and you cannot seem to get a grip on your mind. For the Christian I realized this is a tool the enemy really uses if he can. Beware!

Loneliness. Increased responsibilities and changes in one's life can make you feel lonely and afraid. As you meet new challenges and draw to friends and family that are patient and genuinely concerned, this will fade. There was a short period of which I experienced anxiety, especially at nightfall. I remember once awakening abruptly confused and expecting Ted to be beside me. When I realized what happened I thought, "Alright girlfriend, get a grip."

You will not always want to be around people. Sometimes I needed alone time. Just tell your true friends and kindred to keep their phones handy. Always remember Jesus left us a Comforter who is the Holy Spirit.

Hope. May not seem like it at first but you will reach a stage where you can focus on your future with hope. No matter how difficult life gets during the grieving period you can and will pull through. How? The Joy of the Lord is our strength. God gives us strength to overcome life's obstacles.

The Word Reads:

*Psalm 28:7 The LORD [is] my **strength** and my shield; my heart trusted in him, and I am helped: therefore my heart greatly rejoiceth; and with my song will I praise him.*

*Psalm 29:11 The LORD will give **strength** unto his people; the LORD will bless his people with peace.*

*Psalm 37:39 But the salvation of the righteous [is] of the LORD: [he is] their **strength** in the time of trouble.*

Chapter 7
TAKING CARE OF FINAL MATTERS

During the first hours and days you can expect a considerable amount of activity from friends, family, and neighbors coming to extend their condolences, bringing food or to offer help. Decisions have to be made selecting a mortuary service, casket and clothing for burial if this has not been prearranged.

Taking part in these activities and preparations can be painful and you may just go through the motions due to emotional numbness. Believe it or not, this is all a part of the grieving process. It is important to select beforehand, people who have your best interest at heart if you desire support in these areas. My eldest son actually handled the mortuary portion. I was just there saying, "That's fine," to everything they asked. He even returned to Inglewood Park six weeks later to make sure the name plate was placed and the information was correct.

There may be some important business matters you need to attend to like retaining an attorney, considering the Will and/or Living Trust, and applying for benefits.

Be sure to order additional copies of the Death Certificate to send to various creditors. Applying for benefits may include retirement benefits, Social Security Benefits, Life Insurance policies personal and employee related and Veterans Benefits.

You may find it necessary to change title of ownership on: mortgage, insurance policies, burial property, automobiles, will or living trust, credit cards, bank accounts and stocks, bonds and investments.

It may be wise to prepare a check list now of papers you will need.

Along with copies of the Death Certificate (you can order these through the funeral home or County Health Department) you will need copies of:

- Insurance Policies
- Marriage License
- Dependent Children's birth certificates
- Original Will or Living Trust
- Veteran's certificate or honorable discharge
- Your own Social Security number as well as the deceased and for any dependent children

It is advisable to keep these items in a secure place you can readily access if the time comes. A person grieving does not need the added stress of looking for important documents or wondering what needs to be done next.

We never know what our reaction will be at the time of loss. We would like to think we will have complete control but this but it is not probable. There are usually so many things to be done the more we can preplan the better it will be for us during such a time.

The only preparation we made was the mausoleum, opening and closing cost and name plate, which was better than nothing I suppose. Because of our church affiliation we did not have to worry about a venue for the service. But the burial cost had to be paid with insurance policy or cash and we lacked having a burial policy. I thank God for family, loving pastors, church family and friends.

Through the whole process I was truly blessed and had the favor of God. The representative from the mortuary new Ted and I well so he came to the house with a few packages put together. All my son had to do was, examine them and choose. Notice I said my son. My attitude at that time was...whatever and I trusted my son's judgment and he did a marvelous job, "Thank you Denzil."

Chapter 8
SURVIVING THE LOSS

Will I survive? Ted would want me to. Surrounding myself with wonderful memories and allowing time for the grieving process has been a great healthy beginning for me. Although the simplest things will sometimes trigger tears; reading his Bible, the many pictures we have of vacations taken together, revisiting familiar places, songs on the radio and familiar movies, is all a part of the healing process. Getting my life back which includes doing things alone we did together is a daily effort. Dealing with people questioning me of Ted's whereabouts that were accustomed to seeing us together that was a tough one. For a while I purposely avoided some familiar places because I did not want to explain where he was. But I soon had to face it and go.

A pharmacist who is Christian shared with me that our relationship and my strength caused her to view life differently. She married three months after Ted passed. She told her husband that she no longer wanted a huge house or loads of material possessions. She wanted them to have good health and to live a long healthy life together. She said our lives together changed hers and served as a great example of the beauty of marriage. I praise God that the Jesus in our relationship showed brightly in our daily lives together.

What makes a tremendous difference in a saved person's healing is our relationship with the Father and the hope we have through Jesus Christ…Good God Almighty!

Endurance is a must! There were some people that approached me saying things out of ignorance (I mean no disrespect) regarding my husband's demise while some purposed to try and make me break down and cry. The world is made of all kinds of people and it is no different in ministry.

I discovered the stronger you appear to some when going through life's challenges the more the enemy wants to expose weakness. Our strength through difficult times helps others. To a person grieving, emotions can be such a roller coaster ride it does not register to us as strength or weakness but a period of survival.

Again, no disrespect intended. The Holy Spirit, who guides, corrects and teaches us will never instruct anyone in Christ to say or do something that is against the Word or the Will of God. Knowing this, when people address us, especially during this time they are either operating with the Holy Spirit, in their flesh and some operate because of ignorance (not knowing). You will learn how to disallow people to offend or hurt you this way. Personally, I change the subject, walk away or make an excuse to discontinue the conversation. I simply refuse to allow the enemy to come at me like that.

Be assured as time goes by you will be strengthened and equipped with the tools to control your space when people invade it. It's the insensitive people I avoid, those who do not know what to say and those who do not care about what they say.

Day by day is how I survive. Taking things at my own pace is important and not trying to adjust my life to how others think I should. People and friends mean well but everyone deals with death and grief in their own way. As long as it is in a healthy manner, allow yourself time to grieve and heal. I cannot say this enough but Grief Counseling has been an excellent source of support and I also realize that every positive source is a resource from God. In reality, it will never be over I will learn how to live without Ted and enjoy the memories. Each passing day brings added strength.

Another factor which was and is a tremendous help is working in ministry. There was never any pressure from my pastors and I found later they were a little concerned with me continuing working. I never shared my feelings with members or other leaders but I did talk honestly with my Pastors. At my lowest point people were still looking towards me for strength partially because of my position in the ministry and because I have always been a strong pillar in storms. Parishioners often preconceive that the greater the "title" the stronger the faith should be.

There were a few times I would have a "melt-down" and remained home, but for most services I was in attendance. There was a lot of work because we worked as executive pastors together but I did not mind it because it kept my mind busy and helped me focus.

The fellowship was soothing and comforting to me. It seemed as though God was giving my pastor a message of hope in the preached Word just for me. Currently I am not a member of the church referred to in this book but during the early days we moved to a larger location which was good. The most challenging aspect for me in the old building, was sitting in service without my husband, we always sat and worked together. The new facility gave me as well as my pastors a new beginning.

Removing clothing and personal belongings was another tough one. Suddenly with no warning I wanted to get his belongings out the house. I began emptying closets and drawers stacking everything in another room. Many of his personal things I gave to friends and family. If you recall he was a stylish dresser with no shortage of suits, ties, shoes and shirts. We filled three vehicles including the inside and trunks to transport his things to the Goodwill. I was fine until it was time to unload, thought I was suffocating. My children handled that for me and sent me home. But I did remember to get a receipt because you can use it later for tax purposes.

After a loss, I find it is important to rebuild our lives. It will take courage to take some first steps to engage with life again after a loss. It will be important for you to find ways that work best for you. You may want to:

Take a class: Look at community college, adult education programs and senior centers which can cover any class you can imagine. You may want to learn a music instrument, or become computer savvy, learn another language. There are many things at our disposal we just have to get the interest to do it.

Volunteer Work: Some people find it helpful doing volunteer work. Just call various agencies or surf the internet, check newspapers and ask about volunteer work. Some rehabilitation or skilled nursing facilities need volunteers, animal shelters need volunteers. They even provide a class teaching how to handle animals.

Arts & Sports: There are specific groups that support either artistic or athletic endeavors such as water aerobics, tai chi, dancing, etc. I would take Salsa lessons if my knees did not object.

Participate in a Faith Community: Many receive support by participating in a faith community. In addition to worship experiences these faith communities can provide excellent education and social events. Involvement in ministry has been my life. It was one of the difficult participations to continue. But it is also something we both loved to do. Sometimes there may seem like a small emotional war is brewing. Just when you think you have lost the battle victory is around the corner. Each new victory no matter how small or large to you…is a victory just the same.

In my current ministry I sat almost a year before trying to work. Had a meeting with my pastor and first lady which helped tremendously allowing myself time to heal and regain my focus. Pacing myself, I am slowly getting back into ministry work.

Take a Risk: Engaging socially can be a great help to grieving recovery. You may need to take the first step and invite a friend or neighbor to go shopping, to a movie, go out for a meal, or to take a walk or share another event with you. I took risks. Although they were not easy I conquered the fear of attending functions alone. I went to the movies first alone. Cried through the whole movie but I did it. The movie was not a tear jerker it was an outing we always did together. After I conquered each risky endeavor I would do it a second and third time with my daughter and granddaughter.

If there would be anything I would want you to receive or learn from this book is never take things or people for granted. Enjoy life especially positive relationships.

Take advantage of this life by taking time to fruitfully live it because there are no second chances after death.

I have certainly learned through this experience that expressing my grief had the greatest potential for healing which is strengthening and enriching my life. There is no right or wrong way to grieve — but I have found there are ways to make our grieving more complete and more positive.

With a great entourage of support, I have begun to step back into the stream of life, doing things we loved to do and going places we enjoyed and loved going. My plans are to continuously work on enjoying the rest of my days to live life in the fullest measure.

Norms You Want To Look For in Grief Support Groups
Dr. Roscoe Y. Miller Kaiser Permanente Bereavement Program

1. The group and participates should make every effort to arrive on time and start on time.

2. The facilitators should do their best to make sure everyone has time to share.

3. Please remember it is a process where we support others and not give them advice.

4. The facilitators should work to create a "safe space" where each person can be respected and their pain honored.

5. All should agree to respect one another's confidences by not taking personal information beyond this meeting without permission of those who share with the group.

6. Just as the session begins on time, they should end on time it's not a church meeting.

AM I LOSING MY MIND?
NORMAL GRIEVING SYMPTOMS

Is there a right way to grieve? Why do I feel out of control?

- I feel as if it isn't real ❀
- I feel a tightness in my throat and a heaviness in my chest ❀
- My mood changes over the slightest things ❀
- What is there left to live for? (Saints, we cannot have this thought…bind it and loose it)
- Sometimes I feel angry (But not at God) ❀
- I cry at unexpected times…Melt-downs :)
- I don't want others to see me when I feel sad ❀
- I cannot concentrate
- I sense my loved one's presence, like hearing their voice
- I feel that my mind is on a merry-go-round that will not stop ❀
- I have trouble sleeping (Ohhh yes!) ❀
- I don't feel hungry ❀
- I am eating all the time
- I miss being touched ❀
- I miss having someone help me make decisions ❀
- I am so lonely ❀
- I feel guilty
- I have regrets
- I should have… ❀

It is so very important to reach out and talk with people (you can trust) and to allow yourself to express your feelings and cry when you need to. Be gentle and kind to you. These responses to grief are natural and normal.

❀ My experiences

COPING TOOLS

❀ Remember to take care of "you." When you eat make sure it is healthy food or a supplement.

❀ Find a supportive person or someone you can trust to share your feelings.

❀ Allow yourself time for healing. Its timing cannot be rushed.

❀ When you are experiencing the various emotions it can be confusing.

❀ Maintain a regular schedule as much as possible

❀ Do not make major decisions (moving, large purchases or selling your home).

❀ Avoid unrealistic goals and expectations for yourself.

❀ Make choices that satisfy you. You may not feel like the annual family gathering.

❀ Maintain an awareness of your body's need for nutrition and rest. Listen to the messages your body sends.

❀ If new or unusual symptoms arise, see your physician.

<u>GRIEF CYCLE</u>
Life's Function
Loss
Numbing
Yearning
Disorganization
Despair/Reorganization
Recovery

If you do not go through the cycle through the process of grieving you continue <u>repeating the cycle. When you go through the cycle you reach recovery</u>

<u>Numbing</u>: Shock, confusion, denial, overwhelmed, panic, tense, apprehension, lowered self-esteem, passivity, mechanical functioning, unawareness of others, outbursts.

<u>Yearning</u>: Sadness, pining, anger, stabbing pain, loneliness, guilt, sobbing, hallucination, vivid dreams, ambivalence, physical symptoms, depression.

<u>Despair/Disorganization</u>: Apathy, inability to concentrate, withdrawal, forgetfulness, loss of interest, poor eating and health habits, difficulty with decisions, taking on patient's symptoms, preoccupied with illness/death, worthlessness, suicidal feelings, depression, restlessness.

<u>Reorganization</u>: Ebb and flow of feelings, occasionally peaceful, regained confidence/independence, beginning to feel natural.

HEAVEN'S BEST

Written by: Shiela Y. Harris – September, 2008

While you here with us on earth
You made everyone smile
Pressed untiringly in Kingdom work
Perfection was your style

Your legacy will be remembered
Through music and ministry
Your love of life was an endearment
To all who could see

Your love will always be treasured
God knew you would stand His tests
Your faithfulness cannot be measured
You are one of Heaven's Best

ABOUT THE AUTHOR

Shiela Y. Harris

One of her favorite past times is writing and providing office and graphic services through "The Fantasy Graphics" a home-based business. Another enjoyment is teaching and ministering to the needs of women. During the loss of her husband her membership was with Church of the Word – South Bay where she served as Executive Pastor on the Executive Board and Executive Team of this ministry and her senior and co-Pastors were Henry & Alicia Pigee'. Currently her membership is with Worship Center Community Church – Long Beach, California, a vastly growing ministry with Pastor Sheridan & First Lady Larleslie McDaniel.

Shiela is one of four children and the only girl, the mother of three children; Denzil, Chisa and Damien and a proud grandmother of, Ashley and Trinity. Along with her late husband it was discovered in 2006 he had a twenty-three year old daughter Tony and three beautiful grandchildren, "Q," and twin boys Imari and Amir born in March 2007.

At the onset of this book, Shiela's husband Ted Harris had passed exactly fourteen months prior but he did have the good fortune of seeing her first work, "How to be Free from Excess Baggage."

Well educated Shiela received her BA at Cal State University, Dominguez Hills and a Masters in Ministry at the California School of Ministry, Los Angeles Campus. A long term goal is to pursue her Doctorate in Ministry.

After spending over 20 years in the music ministry God called her to preach and teach the Gospel. It has not been an easy task for her to continue this path without her husband and best friend. They worked closely together in ministry, well over eleven years and both had a "spirit of excellence." It is one of many adjustments we sometimes have to make in life but she is determined to continue doing Kingdom work.

She is a gift to the Body of Christ and community with a lot to offer, through teaching and preaching from personal experiences, practical principals and through Biblical concepts.

RESOURCES

Parents Without Partners – 1-800-637-7974
www.parentswithoutpartners.org

Widowed Persons Service Call: AARP - 1-800 424-3410
http://www.aarp.org/families/grief_loss/

National Mental Health Information Center
http://mentalhealth.samhsa.gov/

National Suicide Prevention Lifeline -1-800-273-TALK (8255)
http://www.suicidepreventionlifeline.org/

Blue Letter Bible.Org, David Guzik Commentary

Eye of the Storm, Wikipedia Online Encyclopedia

Bereavement Support Group,
Publications Kaiser Permanente, Downey CA

BibleStudy.org, Definition of "Rhema."

Insomnia Treatment: Cognitive Behavioral Therapy
Instead of Sleeping Pills, Mayo Clinic.com

Other Teachings....

- ## How to be Free From Excess Baggage

Her first book, for all that take unresolved, emotional issues from one relationship to another. Life's negative experiences resulting from traumas encountered in childhood and as adults are destructive and result in low and no self-esteem ultimately causing chaotic relationships. We learn why and how we take painful experiences into new relationships better known as "excess baggage," and how to get delivered, be free and know it. Useful materials and handouts are provided with this teaching. This is a powerful deliverance ministry.

- ## Ladies, No More Fishing

This is a dynamic teaching targeting women who are seeking God for a mate. She uses biblical and practical principals encouraging women to wait on God to send their mate. When we fish for men we set ourselves up for destructive, unfulfilled, one-sided relationships. Useful materials and handouts are provided with this teaching.

- ## Do Christians Have to Fall

There are many great men and women who have been tricked and fooled by the enemy. Secretly and in the open are caught up in ungodly sinful practices that not only discredit them, but also the Body of Christ. This teaching helps us to understand how and why we fall and also biblically supports that we do not have to. Moreover it teaches how we can keep from falling.

- **Living Saved and Single…**

  For men and women, dating, engaged, divorced, widowed, etc.

- **I'm Grieving and I Can't Get up**

Teaching based on this book, "Surviving the Loss of a Loved One." In a group setting we learn how to understand the grieving process, what to expect during the grieving and how to survive it. As she shares the loss of her husband she is transparent with her emotions throughout the grieving process. This can be very beneficial to your congregation to help those who are caught in the grieving cycle, to go through in a healthy manner and come out healthy and victorious. Also teaches us how to recognize danger symptoms, knowing what to do when they experience "melt downs" and where to look for additional help if needed. Useful materials and handouts are provided with this teaching.

- **Recipe for a Good Marriage**

With divorce as common in the church as in the world, practical principals and Biblical teaching on saving the institution of marriage. What causes marriages to fail? Why are spouses unfaithful? Why do we fall out of love so easy and more? Have men and women's rolls switched or changed? Can spouses be faithful? What does the Bible say about Divorce?

- **Ministering to Your Pastor**

Scriptural and practical teaching why it is important for parishioners to support their ministry and pastor. What happens when we don't support. What does God expect of us?

- ## Recipe for a GREAT Marriage

With divorce as common in the church as in the world, practical principals and Biblical teaching on saving the institution of marriage. What causes marriages to fail? Why are spouses unfaithful? Why do we fall out of love so easy and more? Have men and women's rolls switched or changed? Can spouses be faithful? What does the Bible say about Divorce?

- ## Church Administration & Staff Training

Teaching includes instructions on how to perform in an effective and efficient manner using up-to-date technology, forms control, software and office procedures. Organizing your work and managing your staff.

Elder Shiela Harris is available for teaching, and speaking.
Call Touch the World TV & Artist Management at

213-485-7210 or 562-436-9409

For information and availability

Also see websites at:

http://churchadministrationtraining.webs.com

www.touchingtheworldnow.com

www.ingramcontent.com/pod-product-compliance
Lightning Source LLC
Chambersburg PA
CBHW060427090426
42734CB00011B/2473